LOWER
WENSL

SHORT · SCENIC · WALKS

PAUL HANNON

HILLSIDE PUBLICATIONS
20 Wheathead Crescent
Keighley
West Yorkshire
BD22 6LX

First Published 2010

© Paul Hannon 2010

ISBN 978 1 870141 99 4

*The sketch maps are based on 1947 OS one-inch maps
and earlier OS six-inch maps*

Cover illustration: Jervaulx Abbey
Back cover: Sunset over Penhill
Page 1: River Burn at Low Burn Bridge, Masham
(Paul Hannon/Hillslides Picture Library)

Printed by Steffprint
Unit 5, Keighley Industrial Park
Royd Ings Avenue
Keighley
West Yorkshire
BD21 4DZ

CONTENTS

INTRODUCTION

The broad valley of Wensleydale extends far beyond the Yorkshire Dales National Park, so while a third of these walks are within its boundary, others explore the River Ure through equally rewarding countryside by way of Middleham and Masham to the tiny cathedral city of Ripon. Allied to this, the river's graceful curve embraces an upland scene where rolling moors are drained by the tributary rivers Burn, Laver and Skell. This area, featuring beguiling Colsterdale and Dallowgill, falls within the Nidderdale Area of Outstanding Natural Beauty: within it stands one of the brightest jewels in the Yorkshire crown, Fountains Abbey, whose impressive ruins and beautiful setting are equalled by the adjacent deer park of Studley Royal.

Focal point for the area is the little market town of Leyburn, while delightful villages such as Sawley, Kirkby Malzeard, East Witton, Wensley and West Tanfield abound. The endearing ruins of Jervaulx Abbey concede little to Fountains in their parkland setting, while Middleham Castle is an imposing fortress. The more natural landmark of shapely Penhill overlooks the wild beauty of Coverdale, while Redmire Force and Cover Banks provide beautiful moments. The area is rich in curiosities such as the Druid's Temple at Ilton and the follies of Hackfall Woods, while equally diverse highlights include Eavestone Lake, the Templars' Chapel and the Wensleydale Railway. The upper half of the dale continuing through Aysgarth and Bainbridge to Hawes is the subject of a companion guide to 20 further walks.

The majority of walks are on rights of way with no access restrictions. A couple make use of 'Right to Roam' to cross Open Country: these areas can be closed for up to 28 days each year subject to advance notice, though the small sections in these walks are unlikely to be affected. Many walks can be accessed by public transport, so even if you come to the district by car, consider the local bus in order not to exacerbate congestion. Whilst the route description should be sufficient to guide you around each walk, a map is recommended for greater information: Ordnance Survey 1:25,000 scale maps give the finest detail, and Explorer maps OL30, 298, 299 and 302 cover the walks.

Middleham Castle

USEFUL INFORMATION

·Yorkshire Dales National Park (01756-751600)
·Aysgarth Falls National Park Centre (01969-662910)
·Leyburn Tourist Information (01969-623069)
·Ripon Tourist Information (0845-3890 178)
·Yorkshire Dales Society (01729-825600)
·Open Access (0845-100 3298) www.countrysideaccess.gov.uk
·Traveline - public transport information (0870-6082608)

LOWER WENSLEYDALE

20 Short Scenic Walks

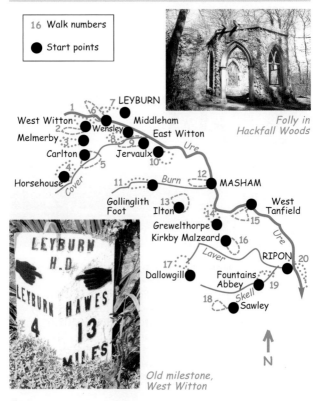

16   Walk numbers

●   Start points

Folly in Hackfall Woods

7 LEYBURN

1

6

West Witton   Middleham
2   Wensley
Melmerby   East Witton
3   8
Carlton   9   Jervaulx
4   5   Ure
Horsehouse   Cover   10

11   Burn   12
Gollinglith   13   MASHAM
Foot   Ilton
Grewelthorpe   14
Kirkby Malzeard   15   West Tanfield
16   Ure
17   Laver   RIPON   20
Dallowgill   Fountains
Abbey   19
18   Skell
Sawley

LEYBURN H.D.

LEYBURN HAWES

4   13

MILES

Old milestone, West Witton

N

A RECORD OF YOUR WALKS

WALK	DATE	NOTES
1		
2		
3		
4		
5		
6		
7		
8		
9		
10		
11		
12		
13		
14		
15		
16		
17		
18		
19		
20		

*4¹2 miles
from West Witton*

**Exploring quiet corners
of the River Ure on
delectable old paths**

Start Village centre
(GR: 061883), roadside parking, lay-by at east end
Map OS Explorer OL30 Yorkshire Dales North/Central

For a note on West Witton see page 10. At the Leyburn end of the village take a walled lane just after the last house on the left. Almost at once fork right on a more inviting enclosed way, Back Lane. On descending note stately Bolton Hall in parkland on the opposite bank: Preston-under-Scar sits high above, while Bolton Castle can be seen to the left. Twisting, turning and narrowing, this mercurial footway leads steadily downhill towards the river. At its demise don't use the gate in front, but opt for a stile on the right. In the field stay close to the left-hand boundary, until it doubles sharply back left at a minor bank above a flat pasture just short of the Ure. Advance a little further then double back across the centre of this flat pasture on a trod to a gate in a wall.

Across the stream behind, ignore a grass track heading away, and drop to a stile onto the riverbank. Plain sailing now ensues as the Ure is accompanied up-dale for a full mile and a half through a succession of quiet pastures. Bolton Castle appears straight ahead, with Penhill near-permanent up to the left. Beyond the large, wooded Batt Island the way forges on over small knolls to reach a tree-clad brow above a sharp, lively bend. Dropping to cross a tiny stream, a wall soon intervenes to deflect you from the river: to your left an alternative grassy path runs on from the stream's spring to meet the wall. Follow it through a pasture of distinctive grassy hummocks to a ladder-stile: it is to this point you will return after visiting Redmire Force. A little path continues through a smaller pasture to a small gate into the wooded environs of the riverbank. A path heads away, and almost immediately Redmire Force greets the eye below: be wary of the steep drop from this vantage point. The splendour of this scene is the scale of the Aysgarth-like falls on this wide section of river, not to mention the wooded surrounds and lack of fellow humans! The continuing path drops to the very edge of the upper fall, your turning point.

Return out of the wood and back towards the ladder-stile, but then veer right to join a parallel grass track: this roughly follows the course of an old route that forded the Ure. It runs on through a gate then crosses a field centre to the foot of Swinithwaite's Back Lane beneath New Wood. From the left-hand gate rise outside the wood: at the top corner Penhill re-appears. Continue to the brow, then on to a bridle-gate in the far corner. Ascend the wallside until a gate near the end marks the start of an enclosed green way. This rises delightfully away, a super course with more big views over the valley. After levelling out the village appears ahead, and after it swings right to rise to the road just ahead, take a stile on the left. Cross the field to one in the facing wall, then slant up the bank to a gate in a small kink near the far end. This sends an enclosed fieldside path away to enter the western end of the village between gardens.

Redmire Force

4¹₄ miles
from West Witton

**Exceptionally easy walking
on Penhill's lower flanks**

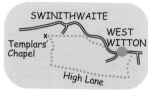

Start Village centre
(GR: 061883), roadside parking, lay-by at east end
Map OS Explorer OL30 Yorkshire Dales North/Central

West Witton is a pleasant village on the slopes of Penhill. It boasts two pubs, the Fox & Hounds and the Wensleydale Heifer, and a Post office/store. The village is perhaps best known for the annual burning of Bartle, when an effigy is gleefully burnt in Guy Fawkes fashion. This occurs near St Bartholomew's feast day in late August. Bartle is said to have been a local sheep thief who was hounded across the flanks of Penhill: a mosaic trail has recently been created to trace the course of the chase. St Bartholomew's church is tucked secretively away down a back lane: dating largely from mid-Victorian times it retains a 16th century tower. There is a Wesleyan Chapel of 1842 with a Sunday School of 1884 attached.

Leave by the public garden opposite the Wensleydale Heifer: by the little pond a snicket takes up between high walls to emerge into a field. Bear left to a stile, then slant up to a gate/stile in the next hedge. Don't take it but turn up to the top corner. A stile admits into trees and a path slants up the bank. At the top is a fork: go left a few yards to a stile, then continue away with a line of trees to the head of the grassy way of Watery Lane. From a stile opposite, cross the field to a corner stile alongside a tiny stream and rise steeply with it to a stile onto High Lane. Turn right along the firm track of this old walled road: virtually dead-flat, it remains underfoot for a good 1¹₂ miles. Viewed across the dale are Castle Bolton, Redmire, Preston-under-Scar and Leyburn Shawl.

At a junction with a similar lane from the right turn to look up at the scarred face of Penhill, set back much higher above. Turn right on this lane, level for a while before the walls diverge and it winds steeply down past an old quarry with big valley views. At a sharp right bend above a wood, bear left on a grassy track, quickly slanting right off it down to a gate at the left edge of the wood. In the pasture below is the Templars' Chapel, and a fading grassy track drops down to the head of a walled lane alongside it. The chapel of the Knights Templar is less exciting than it looks on the map. The low ruins of the chapel of the Penhill Preceptory date from the early 13th century and include several graves: adjoining buildings remained uncovered when this was excavated in 1840.

Leave by doubling back right with the wall above the wooded bank, the start of an extended level stroll interrupted only by crossing a firm, enclosed track further on: several wall-stiles are encountered. A brief open section exploits views to Castle Bolton, Preston and Redmire beneath their scars beyond Swinithwaite Hall directly below you. Reaching a stile onto the main road, don't use it but bear right up to one in the wall ahead. The dark wall of Penhill rises steeply above you now. Bear right across the brow to the far corner where a stile admits to the right edge of a small wood. Emerging at the other side go on a short way to a gap-stile before the corner, emerging alongside a horse-training establishment. From a corner stile to the left cross a field to find a stile onto the road at the edge of West Witton. Turn right to enter the village.

The Templars' Chapel

11

*3¾ miles
from Melmerby*

**A high-level start to a
memorable ascent of
Wensleydale's favourite hill**

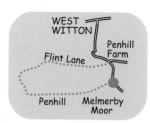

Start **Melmerby Moor (GR:
067868), parking area on road summit above cattle-grid**
Map OS Explorer OL30 Yorkshire Dales North/Central
Access Open Access, see page 4

After admiring Penhill End with its prominent cairn across the moor, turn down the West Witton road, over the cattle-grid off the moor and down to Penhill Farm. At the junction here turn left along the enclosed track of Flint Lane, with views over West Witton to much of Wensleydale, backed by a long moorland skyline. Follow this green lane all the way to its terminus, a splendid stride with Penhill's long, rugged wall above. Emerging through a gate at the end the track continues along a wallside, passing through a gate in it near the end to enter the open country of Penhill Quarry.

While the main track remains with the wall, take a lesser but clear one rising very gently left towards a line of spoil heaps, crossing a couple of thinner paths to rise as a sunken way above the furthest one. It continues a little further then doubles back uphill to commence a surprisingly easy climb: this expertly engineered sunken way was built to transport sleds of peat from the moor, and rises with one sharp zigzag to the edge of Penhill's summit plateau, with Black Scar to the right and Penhill Scar left. Ignore the gate and turn left along the wall to a stile, continuing on a sketchy path along the edge. The Ordnance Survey column stands over the wall as you forge on to drop gently to another stile where a sturdy wall crumbles away down the bouldery scarp. Just two minutes further is the raised mound of the beacon site: from here the tip of the big cairn on Penhill End can be seen, and a broad path bears right to it. A fine feature of this view is the full length of Coverdale leading the eye to Great Whernside overtopping Little Whernside.

Penhill is Wensleydale's best-known fell, its abrupt northern edge rendering it identifiable from much of the dale, and it is a regular feature of views west from the North York Moors. Penhill's own virtues as a viewpoint are assisted by the dramatic plunge of the Scar, which provides near bird's-eye pictures of the lower dale. It is the aforementioned advantages which have given the hill historical significance: it was the site of a beacon, one of a chain which when lit rapidly spread warning of impending danger such as the Spanish Armada. Less certain is that it was also an Iron Age chieftain's burial site. Strictly speaking, the true summit is a mile south-west of the Ordnance column. To clarify what exactly is what on the summit plateau, the true top is 1814ft/553m, the OS column is 1725ft/526m, and the beacon site is 1684ft/514m.

Your descent bridleway should be very clear as it drops to run through pastures below. A broad path drops directly from the cairn to the first gate, initially steeply then merging into the bridleway, the self-explanatory Middleham Peat Road. Through the gate the track begins a splendid march gently down through a string of gates in parallel walls, only fading in the final field. Keep straight on, passing an old bield (sheep shelter) to reach a gate back onto the road with the cattle-grid just yards to your right.

Penhill from Melmerby Moor

4¾ miles
from Horsehouse

Charming river and rough pasture surrounding a remote hamlet

Start Village centre (GR: 047813), roadside parking
Map OS Explorer OL30 Yorkshire Dales North/Central

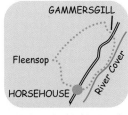

GAMMERSGILL

Fleensop

River Cover

HORSEHOUSE

Horsehouse is the first sizeable community in Coverdale, its grey buildings huddled around the cosy Thwaite Arms. St Botolph's church dates from 1869, while on the road up-dale is a former Wesleyan chapel of 1828. Go left on an access lane behind the pub, soon leaving it down a small lawn to a gate below. Descend a small enclosure to a gate into fields, bearing left to another gate and on to a hand-gate right of a barn. The River Cover is now joined and, ignoring an early footbridge and later an arched farm bridge, is traced downstream for a mile. Part way through this you emerge via a sidestream into a large open pasture: remain on the open bank, curving increasingly pleasantly around with a wooded bank opposite. After a gate/stile at the end, vacate it at a second solitary stile, crossing diagonally to a gate/stile in line with a lone house. Continue towards the house, bearing further right to a hand-gate. A part wooded enclosure leads onto the road in the hamlet of Gammersgill.

Go right on the road out, and after the last house take a gate on the left where a grassy track crosses to a gate in the far wall. Entering a sloping pasture go right on this wallside track, rising gently to the far corner. Don't pass through but double back left up the steep slope, rising to a gate/stile in a fence. Big views now look back over the dale. With a wood to your right, resume climbing past a wall end and up to a skyline barn. To its left is a stile, from where continue past a second barn to a brow beyond. Now drop left to a tiny sidestream, with tree-lined Turn Beck down to your right. Rise to a wall-stile just above, and a thin trod heads off, wall and stream converging at the end. Here use a stile by an old gate on the left.

A thin path rises onto grassy moor, a delightful stride shadowing the stream down to your right. At the end this fades as you reach a gate/stile ahead. Bear a little left through dry reeds and resume on a gentle brow, a thin path continuing to a ladder-stile in the next wall. Views down-dale look to the Scrafton moors and Great Roova Crags. Now drop left to pick up a grassy track running left to a gate in a wall. Through it go right to a gate at the far end and follow a fence away towards barns. Drop left to a gate beyond the nearest one, and head away on its access track. This runs into the Fleensop Valley to approach the farm at Fleensop. Crossing Fleemis Gill, double back left on the surfaced road away from the farm, and rising away, quickly leave it at a gate in the adjacent wall.

Ascend the steep pasture to a stile at the top-left corner above a conifer block. A grassy wallside path then ascends rough moorland through dry reeds. Just short of the top the path veers right to gain the ridge wall as a broad track comes down from the right. Little and Great Whernsides appear at the dalehead, which itself rapidly unfolds. Through the gate an intermittent track heads away through reeds. As they fade it drops more markedly through moor-grass as the valley floor returns to view. Between closer walls a clearer way forms, dropping left to slant pleasantly down to a corner gate/stile. An enclosed way now drops infallibly by a wooded beck to emerge quite suddenly back into Horsehouse.

The Thwaite Arms, Horsehouse

4³⁄4 miles
from Carlton

**A delightful amble through
peaceful lower Coverdale**

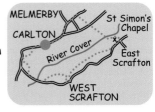

Start Village centre
(GR: 068847), car park
Map OS Explorer OL30 Yorkshire Dales North/Central

Carlton-in-Coverdale is a long, straggly village with many attractive cottages, the Foresters Arms pub, a tiny church and a Methodist chapel. A grassy knoll behind the pub is the site of an early wooden castle. From the village hall head up the main street past the pub. Shortly after, a footpath goes off left along a drive at a tiny sloping green. As the drive ends at the end of the houses take a stile on the left. Here you are immediately out in the open, with a long wall of moorland stretching across the other side of the valley, leading from the Scrafton moors and Great Roova Crags up towards the Whernsides at the dalehead. Head across the field to the next stile, continuing through a handful of gap-stiles to emerge onto a road. Without treading tarmac take a gate on the left to descend to a stile at the bottom. Bear right from this to a corner stile, then on the fieldside to join Cover Lane.

Turn down to Nathwaite Bridge on the River Cover. Two minutes up the other side take a gate on the left, and through one behind slant across the field to a stile at the bottom of a short wall. Look back to a fine prospect of Penhill high above Carlton. Advance along the fence to a gate in it, then slant up to a stile in a fence near the top. Continue up to a wall above, where a kissing-gate sends a path towards West Scrafton. At the corner turn right on a walled green way, emerging onto the end of an access road in the village. Though your onward route is left, first enjoy a small loop by turning right to the through road, then left to a tiny green. West Scrafton is well off the beaten track: the green sits amongst attractive houses and a little Methodist Chapel of 1866.

At the far corner of the green an access track ends in a grassy area between houses, and a path drops right into Caygill Scar's wooded ravine. Over a footbridge on a mill-cut it emerges back where you came in. Turn right on the access track, and a path drops right to rejoin Caygill, through a stile and tracing the gill to a farm bridge. Cross this and a field to a stile onto a corner of an enclosed track, Low Lane. Meeting it at a junction with a sunken way, rise right a few yards to the lane proper and bear left as it rises gently away, improving into a fine green way. At its demise keep straight on the fieldside through a gateway, and cross to a gate ahead. Now bear right to a stile in a tiny section of wall in the corner, then sharp right to a similar arrangement, with gate, at a tiny tree-lined stream. Across, contour left over the field to a footbridge on wooded Thorow Gill. Bear right across the field beyond to a stile onto a road.

Go left to a junction with East Scrafton access road: on the left a stile points down a fieldside to a gate into the Cover's wooded banks. A stepped path drops to the river, past a kiln to the 600-year old ruin of St Simon's Chapel. A path heads upstream past the spring of St Simon's Well, and by low scars to a footbridge on the river. On the other side go right a few yards to a path doubling back up Scar Wood. From a stile at the top rise left to a stile, and up two fields to a road. Go right several yards to a gate, and up the field to Middlefields Farm. A stile right of the barns puts you onto a track, going left on it past the buildings up to a higher road. Turn left past two junctions, the second at the foot of the farming settlement of Melmerby. Keep on to another junction at the start of Carlton.

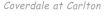

Coverdale at Carlton

4 miles from Wensley

A splendid riverbank and interesting estate grounds

Start Village centre (GR: 091896), roadside parking
Map OS Explorer OL30 Yorkshire Dales North/Central

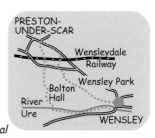

PRESTON-UNDER-SCAR

Wensleydale Railway

Wensley Park

Bolton Hall

River Ure

WENSLEY

Wensley is a delightful village, once an important market town until decimated by the Plague in 1563. The Holy Trinity's Scrope memorials include their late 17th century family pew: also of interest is an early 16th century rood screen. The graceful bridge dates back to the 15th century, though since enlarged. Village pub is the Three Horseshoes, and there is a candle-makers in the old mill. A tiny green featuring a water pump fronts the drive to Bolton Hall. Across the bridge a stile on the right puts you into trees: a good path heads upstream, though the Ure isn't immediately obvious. Beyond a pond the path and river meet to commence a splendid, extended walk through the trees. As the twin-arched Lords Bridge appears ahead the path is deflected left up the bank to a gate/stile, to continue along a fieldside to a gate/stile onto a driveway, Bay Bolton Avenue. Penhill rises boldly up to the left.

Though the next few steps are not an official right of way, it has long been in common use by walkers, courtesy of the landowner: turning right down this takes you across the elegant sloping bridge, with Bolton Hall framed imposingly ahead. On its far side another public footpath is joined, and follows the track which swings left to curve around to a crossroads with a firm driveway. Advance straight up this past Home Farm, bearing left at the top and then continuing uphill at a junction to rise to a road opposite a house at Stoneham. During this spell Addlebrough features in big views up-dale. Cross straight over and up steps to a small gate into a field, with Preston-under-Scar outspread ahead. Cross to a gate accessing the preserved Wensleydale Railway in a minor cutting.

Across, bear left up the field to a stile left of a barn, then left again to find a stile in front of modern houses at the top corner. A snicket rises onto a drive and thence the road. Preston is an unassuming place, with a tiny triangle of green watched over by St Margaret's church, almost lost in a row of houses. Set back is a hall dedicated to the six parishioners who fell in the First World War. Turn right on the side road (not the Richmond road rising away) to leave the village above a wooded bank. With Penhill and Braithwaite Moor well seen ahead, the road drops more steeply to arrive at the beautifully converted, three-storey Preston Mill. Just beyond, a drive comes in from the left: a glance beyond it reveals a tall, square chimney at Keld Head lead smelting mill. From a gate on the right cross to the railway: to the left is the former station.

A path crosses the field behind onto another road. Go briefly left then take a path right into trees. Quickly meeting a driveway junction, go straight ahead on the one leaving the wood. It runs along above the wood top to approach a house. Don't cross the cattle-grid but deflect a few yards left up to a fence corner. Yards further a bridle-gate sends a path down outside the grounds of the house to another such gate into the expanse of Wensley Park, in the grounds of Bolton Hall. The invisible path slants gently down the parkland pasture, ultimately gaining the main drive at a bridle-gate just short of the far corner. Go left to the road in Wensley. Quoits pitches and an ornate lodge are passed at the end.

Preston Mill

19

*4¹2 miles
from Leyburn*

PRESTON
-UNDER
-SCAR   Leyburn Shawl

Tullis Cote   LEYBURN

**Very easy walking
giving outstanding
   views from a wooded limestone escarpment**

Start **Town centre (GR: 112904), ample parking**
Map **OS Explorer OL30 Yorkshire Dales North/Central**

     The busy little town of Leyburn is Wensleydale's true gateway: focal point is a vast market place which still serves its function on Fridays, when dalesfolk from miles around add further colour. At the top stands the imposing town hall of 1856, while ample pubs and cafes do brisk trade. Just off the market place are 18th century Leyburn Hall, Thornborough Hall, enlarged in 1863, St Matthew's church of 1868, and the relatively early Roman Catholic church of St Peter & St Paul, dating from 1835. There is a Tourist Information Centre, and the Wensleydale Show takes place in August.
     Leave the market place by the old town hall, crossing the top road to Commercial Square, with the Bolton Arms on the left. At the top of the small square, 'Way to the Shawl' signs send you up a side street, turning left at the top to emerge via a kissing-gate into the edge of a field. Head away along the forming grassy edge, the start of the Shawl. Leyburn Shawl was laid out as a place of promenade in 1841, a typical Victorian Sunday afternoon attraction. Mary, Queen of Scots was allegedly recaptured here after a brief freedom Bolton Castle. This initial stretch is popular with dog walkers, while there are seats galore from which to appraise the immediate view of Penhill across the dale.
     Advance along the edge, modest limestone outcrops appearing as the path runs on through several fields above the woods. On entering the trees the finest, long section now begins, enjoying panoramic views over the dale. The situation constantly improves as a sheer escarpment beneath your feet creates breaks

over the trees to make more of the view. The presence of a vast quarry over to the right is largely immaterial thanks to a high wall. Old gateposts and a gap-stile at a pronounced gap in the scarp see an old way come slanting up: this is how you will rejoin the Shawl on your return. Eventually the trees, and with them the Shawl end. The path drops down to a stile and kissing-gate out into a large sloping pasture, with truly spacious views looking to Penhill and beyond. Slant down the field to a kissing-gate at the bottom, then across to another. Bear left to a nearby fence corner enclosing the banks and ditches of an ancient settlement and field system. A track forms to turn down through a gate in the wall below, and runs down to a junction with a firmer track above Tullis Cote Farm.

This is your turning point, so double back left on the level track along the bottom of four fields, with the Shawl looking good ahead. Emerging into a much larger sloping pasture, bear left across 'ridge and furrows' towards the top corner. Making for the first scrubby tree a trod forms, becoming a better path to climb to the wall at the foot of Warren Wood. It slants up beneath the wood, through a gate/stile where the finest place for a longer sojourn may delay you before rejoining the outward route. All that remains is to retrace steps through the opening mile and a half.

The return path, Leyburn Shawl

3¾ miles from Middleham

A short ramble to an old hamlet from a unique moor patrolled by racehorses

MIDDLEHAM

Middleham Low Moor

Pinker's Pond

Thorngill

Coverham

Bird Ridding

Cover

Start Pinker's Pond (GR: 114869), roadside parking area a mile south-west of town on Middleham Low Moor
Map OS Explorer OL30 Yorkshire Dales North/Central

Cross towards the regularly dry hollow of Pinker's Pond, but turn up a grass track that served the quarry just above. It turns right beneath the quarry, but leave by a thin path at the end, rising to a fence-end above. Now go left on a fence-top trod that runs beyond its other end to enjoy a superb section above the rim of the scarp of Ever Bank, looking down on the pond and across to Braithwaite Moor, Coverdale and Penhill. At the end it fades on nearing a wall: bear right to its top corner, above which a firm track runs. You are now virtually on the crest of Middleham Low Moor. Either go left with this track, or strike off across the short-cropped grass. An Ordnance Survey column at 774ft/236m soon appears ahead, and is quickly attained. Middleham is renowned for its horse-racing connections and the moor is a favourite venue for putting these graceful animals through their paces.

Ahead the moor stretches out, with Coverdale and Wensleydale divided by Penhill. A gentle drop precedes a steady amble along. With a pronounced dip forming on the left side, drop to rejoin the track by a clump of scrub: alongside is the first chink in the armour of the wall enclosing Cotescue Park, a gate framed by ornate posts and much used for access from the stables below. Turn down this between walls, passing the large house of Fern Gill and with a wooded gill alongside, briefly down its drive: reaching a pond at the start of a wall, go left of the pond across the grounds to a fence-stile opposite. The next stage incorporates a 2010

22

diversion: if for some reason this didn't happen then you would bear right towards Thorngill and follow the old path between the buildings and down to the road. The replacement crosses to the far corner of the field, beyond the last building. Passing through gates bear right to one in the smaller field corner just beyond. Here a grass track is joined, and with Braithwaite Moor outspread ahead, descends a superb fieldside course all the way down onto a road.

Go briefly left to a footbridge on the right, and from a stile behind turn right to trace the wooded stream to a brow at the end, revealing the River Cover down to your left. A track runs on this neck of land, on emerging bear left to a gate onto the access road to Bird Ridding Farm. Go briefly left, and take an inviting enclosed footway after the first house. This drops to the wooded banks of the Cover, a delightful corner. Over a footbridge at the ford of Bird Ridding Wath, the way rises splendidly up the other side onto a back road. Go left for a pleasant half-mile, the wooded bank ushering the Cover in before dropping to Coverham Bridge. Go left over its graceful arch, then look through a gate set back on the right to view an old entrance arch and further scant remains of Coverham Abbey, founded by Premonstratensian canons but within private grounds. On your left a path rises from a gate to Coverham's redundant church of the Holy Trinity. Go left on its pathway out onto a road junction, then turn right to trace Coverham Lane back to the start, rising to regain the moor just short of the pond.

Coverham from the south

23

*4¹⁄4 miles
from East Witton*

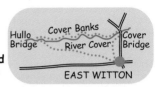

**Easy walking on the wooded
banks of the lower Cover**

Start **Village centre (GR: 144860), roadside parking**
Map **OS Explorer 302, Northallerton & Thirsk
Explorer OL30 Yorkshire Dales North/Central**

East Witton is an early 19th century estate village. Rows
of houses stand back from a vast green, which features a quoits
pitch. At the main crossroads stands the Blue Lion pub, with the
church of St John the Evangelist close by. Leave the far end of the
green on a narrow road, and almost at once take a stile by a gate
on the right. Bear left to a stile at the far end, continuing with a
hedge on the right through two more fields to join grassy West Field
Lane. Turn right on this leafy pathway to it demise at a small wood.
From a stile in front a path runs along the left side of the wood.

Emerging into a field at the end advance straight on: at
the next gate a farm track forms. When it turns left through a
gate to approach East Witton Lodge, leave it and stay on another
wallside track. Penhill is ahead, with Braithwaite Moor to the left.
A gate at the end puts you into open pasture: remain with a hedge
on the right. When this kinks, slant across to rejoin it and stay with
it past a small farm building to pass through the old hedge further
along. On the other side continue on to a stile in the very corner,
and a footbridge crosses a tiny stream into a big pasture. A faint
trod bears right over the centre, crossing to a gate in the opposite
corner. Now overlooking the River Cover, advance on the wooded
bank top high above the river, and towards the end drop down to
stone-arched Hullo Bridge. This sits among splendid scenery as the
river carves a modest ravine and over a slabby limestone bed.

Across it head downstream, and almost at once the path
climbs the wooded bank into a field. Resume on the bank top all the
way to rise to a slim plantation. Twin stiles send a path through it to

resume on the wood top. As it starts to drop back to the river bear left to contour across to a wall/fence opposite, in front of a small wooded gill. Meeting a clear path at a junction turn right, dropping almost to the river. It becomes more wooded at the bottom as the river rolls beneath Cover Scar. Before the bottom a path bears left to slant down to a lower one just above the river. Heading downstream the path soon enters woodland, then climbs above the river before dropping back to leave the wood for open pasture. On the bank a good path re-forms to enter a shorter woodland stretch by the rocky bank. This soon emerges to run to stepping-stones offering a short-cut to East Witton. Resume down your bank to a stile in front, soon after which a stile puts you into the wooded riverbank. The path clings enjoyably to the river to reach the homely Cover Bridge Inn, where you are deflected left to a stile onto the road.

Cross Cover Bridge and take steps on the right down to the river. Cross a stile onto the very bank opposite the pub, but instead of following the Cover upstream, stay with the hedge as it curves left. Go on to a gate/stile at the end, then on to another gate/stile just ahead. Here a guidepost sends a path right towards the stepping-stones, but your way heads directly on, through a gate in a fence and on to a stile by a barn. From a stile round the back go left with the wall. Maintain this line until on a minor brow East Witton appears. In a smaller enclosure take a stile on the left at the end of the hedge, and head along the last field to emerge back into the village alongside an old Methodist chapel of 1882.

East Witton

4¹⁄4 miles from Jervaulx

A ruined abbey in a beautiful setting and a charming village

Start **Abbey tearooms (GR: 169856), car park**
Map **OS Explorer 302, Northallerton & Thirsk**

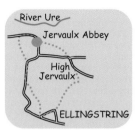

River Ure

Jervaulx Abbey

High Jervaulx

ELLINGSTRING

At the car park are tearooms, crafts, gifts and WCs. From the entrance turn left on the road, initially with a sound path. When a footpath departs right at a bridge you must tramp the verge a short way, until a bridleway departs through a gate on the left just before the adjacent trees end. A faint grassy track heads away with a fence, curving around into the wooded confines of Lea Gill Beck. A modern bridge has replaced the stone-arched casualty alongside, across which a firm track rises to Low Newstead Farm. Turn left on the short drive out onto the bend of a road. Turn right, up the increasing gradients of Stark Bank Road for half a mile.

Reaching a brief pause at the drive to High Newstead Farm on the left, take a stile alongside and cross the field to a gate in the top corner. Maintain the slant to a small gate in the fence ahead (not quite as per map), looking down on the farm. Again slant up to a stile in the top corner onto an access road not on the map. From a stile opposite slant up the field, up a hedgeside to a gate at the top. Now advance to Angram Cote Farm, passing straight through to rise onto a road. In front is an arch-headed well. Turn left a few strides then double back down the road into the lovely little village of Ellingstring, off the beaten track beneath extensive moorland. Alongside a sloping green with seats and daffodils, the old school still sports its bell. Just past a former Wesleyan Methodist chapel of 1848 is Lilac Cottage, for decades an old fashioned youth hostel.

Turn left on an enclosed driveway to Ruskill Bank Farm just before the Victorian postbox. Quickly forking in front of the farm buildings, take the left branch which runs a pleasant hedgerowed course, down to terminate at a choice of gates. Yours is the one on the left just before the track's true demise. Head away, within a few strides bearing right to a bridle-gate. Continue diagonally away from this, on through a hedge-gap before starting a steeper drop. Maintain the slant, dropping by the remains of a hedge, with a sunken way, to a fence corner below. Continue along the fence to a bridle-gate at the very end. Don't pass through, but drop left to a ladder-stile over the wall in the corner. Head away with a tall hedge to a stile onto the A6108 at High Jervaulx Farm: the home of Brymor ice cream has an ice cream parlour and coffee shop.

Follow the road further left to drop to a junction with a side road, escaping through a gate in front into Jervaulx Park. An inviting grass track heads away, and although this runs on to join a firmer carriageway, the right of way bears left of the grass track, keeping a little higher as it runs on to a fence corner, on past trees and a couple of houses before a gentle drop to meet the carriage-way further along, with super views of the abbey. Jervaulx Abbey is in private hands, admission by means of a honesty box. Founded by Cistercian monks in 1156, the name derived from Yore Vale, Yore being the old name for Ure. The remains are less uniform than those under official stewardship, some being totally draped in flowers. The carriageway crosses the visitors' footpath, and in front of Jervaulx Hall (Old Hall), swings left out to the road and car park.

At Jervaulx Abbey

*4½ miles
from Gollinglith Foot*

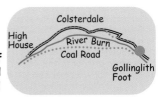

**The unfrequented valley of
the River Burn is savoured
along a classic green road**

Start **Phone box (GR: 153809), parking area
(off Masham-Lofthouse road half-mile west of Healey)**
Map **OS Explorer 302, Northallerton & Thirsk
Explorer OL30 Yorkshire Dales North/Central**

Unless the River Burn is very low, eschew the ford in
favour of a footbridge from the corner of the parking area. From
it turn upstream, past an attractively located cottage to rejoin the
road from the ford: this at once becomes a track, on through a
gate to run past a farm. Ignore the turn into the farm, and as the
old road swings left just beyond, advance through a gate in front
to begin a long march along the Coal Road. The Coal Road runs a
magnificent route along the south side of Colsterdale, a gem of an
old way largely untarnished by modern-day use: truly a classic.

Colsterdale was exploited for coal by the monks of
Jervaulx Abbey, who were granted mining rights by the influential
landowners the Scropes in 1334, and it was still being mined until
much more recent times. The Coal Road lives up to its name by giving
access to long defunct pits in the upper reaches of the River Burn.
Glorious panoramas reveal much of the Colsterdale scene. During
these early stages enjoy the especially rich colour of Birk Gill
Wood in the side valley opposite. Above, and more prominent, are
Slipstone Crags fronting Agra Moor and the bracken-clad moorland
of Long Side. Looking enviably resplendent are scattered farms and
cottages amid the fields immediately across your own valley.

The track levels out at a grassed-over pit, becoming
more exquisite as the immediate surrounds turn as colourful as the
valley scenes. Through the next gate heather takes over alongside

a line of gnarled hawthorn, and the entire scene takes on a wilder mantle as the dalehead appears. At the next gate open country is entered and the now more standard track forges on. Eventually the first farm in the valley, aptly named High House, appears on the opposite bank. The track drops towards it, where a stone bridge arches the Burn, at last seen again in the flesh. This is the walk's turning point, but first advance a short way further. Upstream the main track passes through a gate warning of old mine workings: at this point a grassy path bears right to find the Burn tumbling through a narrow rocky passage. This grassy sward makes a lovely spot to linger by the sparkling stream.

　　　Return to the bridge and cross to the farm, turning right through it to double back down the valley on its access road. Though tarmac, this makes a delightful return journey, gaining some height along the valley flank and offering further lovely views. After dropping close by the beck it rises again slightly to a tract of open country: after a short while look out for a thin path slanting right through bracken to a stile in a gateway in a descending wall. Pass to the right of the bungalow garden at Body Close and join the grassy driveway at the other side, running out to rejoin the road at the foot of a hairpin bend. Resume along the road, this final half-mile being a traffic-free delight in the company of the Burn.

Colsterdale from the Coal Road

29

4³4 miles from Masham

**Easy rambling in the gentle
countryside of the Burn:
some delightful riverbanks**

Start Town centre (GR:
225807), parking in square

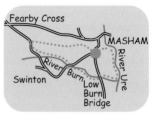

Fearby Cross

MASHAM

River Burn

River Ure

Swinton

Low
Burn
Bridge

Map OS Explorer 298, Nidderdale
Explorer 302, Northallerton & Thirsk

    Masham is a splendid small town, its massive market square
lined by shops, cafes, pubs and cottages: at one corner is St Mary's
church with a 15th century spire. Market days are Wednesday and
Saturday. Masham has long been a brewing centre, and is home to
that Dales icon Theakstons and more recently Black Sheep: both
breweries have visitor centres. A steam rally is held in July, and a
sheep fair in September. Leave the market place by Church Street,
at the opposite side to the church! At a bend at Park Square turn
briefly right then left on a snicket. At the end this emerges onto
Westholme Road at Theakston's Brewery. Go right past the entrance
and along the suburban street. At the sharp bend at the end go
left over an arched bridge, and along a lane past a feeds mill. This
ends when the mill does, continuing as a grassy cart track between
hedgerows. Opening out into a field continue along the hedgeside,
narrowing to a path beyond ramshackle barns to a gate at the end.
    Through this turn sharp left over a stream and along a
grass track to a gate, then bear slightly right across the field to a
stile ahead. Bear right around the field, rejoining the grassy fieldside track to a corner gate. Though the track crosses the field
centre, your way remains with the hedge on the right to a corner
stile, swinging round the corner again and along to emerge onto a
back road, Mickleby Lane. Turn down this for a minute, then go left
through a gate. A grassy track follows the hedgeside to a gate
alongside a small plantation, just past which Shaws Farm appears.
Bear right towards it, encountering a stile before reaching the farm.

Advance into the yard at the rear, but bear left around the buildings on a fieldside to join a track coming out from the farm. This runs above a wooded bank dropping to the River Burn. When the track fades through a gate, bear right down the declining bank to the river. Just beyond, a gate admits to the edge of a golf course. Forge straight on the side of the course, keeping faith with the Burn. Ultimately the path is deflected by the clubhouse to a gate onto a road alongside a stone-arched bridge. Cross it to a stile on the left and resume down the other bank of the river. The golf course remains, though beyond a stile a recommended riverside path keeps you off it. The riverbank path is grand as you advance downstream, the Burn being good company as it leads to an eroded bend. Around it, the way drops to cross a colourful pasture to a stile onto the road at Low Burn Bridge, the well-named final bridge on the Burn.

Cross the bridge and turn downstream on a lovely path between hedgerow and wooded bank. At the end the confluence with the Ure is unseen as a few steps take the path up to the bank of the principal river. The conclusion is a delectable path upstream with the wide-flowing Ure. The church spire remains a permanent feature now to draw you back to the square. This comes beyond a hedgerowed spell at the end, as the path is deflected from the river by the sewage works, and an access track takes over to cross the Glebe, past Mill House and up Millgate into the market place.

The River Ure at Masham

4¹⁴ miles from Ilton

**An amazing folly and a
colourful side valley amid an
elegant country landscape**

*Start Knowle Lane (GR: 177786),
car park a mile north-west of
hamlet at top of unsigned Knowle Lane on Healey-Ilton road
Map OS Explorer 298, Nidderdale (and 302, barely!)*

Saving the Druid's Temple for the end, return a short
way down Knowle Lane to a stile on the left. Cross the field to a gap
in the plantations where elaborate gateposts suggest redundant
stones from the temple. Healey and Fearby villages are seen across
the valley side beyond, with Low Knowle Farm in an attractive landscape below. Through the gate go left outside the plantation on an
embanked green way to a similar break halfway down. A track
comes up from the farm, and once through, turn down the field with
the track dropping to a gate/stile. This superb grassy rake enjoys
extensive views over the Leighton district to Colsterdale's distant
moors, while Leighton Reservoir shimmers ahead.

From the stile head diagonally left across the field to a
stile in a descending fence, in the far corner above a small group of
trees: note the old boundary dyke at this corner. Continue away,
dropping to the edge of a steeper wooded bank above Pott Beck.
Here a grassy track forms, but rather than descending with it,
double back right on its improving course across the field to a gate
above a corner of Hall Wood. This same track now leads pleasantly
on through numerous fields, a straight, level course with excellent
views over the valley of the River Burn on your left, and looking
back up to Colsterdale and across to the small village of Healey. At
the end it reaches the former farm of Broadmires, and follow its
drive out to become a surfaced road before reaching a junction
with the Healey-Ilton road.

Go left, dropping gently down just as far as Stonefold Farm drive on your right. Rising to the yard, enter a small enclosure on the left after the house, then cross to a stile out. Rise a short way with a fence to a stile in it, then bear right across to a gate/stile. Maintain this line to a gate to approach the side valley of Sole Beck Gill, bear right across the field to a gate in a fence, then slant down towards the beck at the bottom corner of a plantation. A stile on the left sends a short path towards the beck, across to another stile, with a ford/footbridge just beyond. Across this the path forks: take the right-hand stile and turn upstream, an improving track running a delightful course along the floor of this colourful little valley all the way to emerge onto a road alongside a barn.

Go very briefly left to an enclosed track right, soon breaking free to run as a green way outside the plantation. At a gate ignore a stile into the trees and turn up the far side of the wall. A grass track climbs two fields to High Knowle. From a stile at the top go left outside the buildings and yard, and through a gate join its drive, rising to emerge onto Knowle Lane. Turn left back to the car park, and a gate sends a broad track into Druid's Plantation, within five minutes reaching the star attraction. The Druid's Temple is a folly constructed in 1820 by William Danby of Swinton Hall, as a useful way of employing his men. The full complement of standing stones is based on the real thing at Stonehenge. Numerous other stone edifices are also spread about the woods.

The Druids' Temple

4¹2 miles from Grewelthorpe

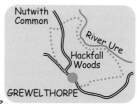

**Restored follies in beautiful
woodland above the Ure**

Start Village centre
(GR: 231761), roadside parking
Map OS Explorer 298, Nidderdale

Grewelthorpe is a linear village with the Crown Inn amid neat cottages. Leave the eastern end beyond the pond: as the road narrows to leave, a hedgerowed cart track leaves a gate on the left. This drops to swing right to a field, but from a gate in front a better green way runs a super enclosed course. At the end ignore a gate in front and take a stile on the right to resume along the hedge. From a stile at the end cross to one in a facing hedge, then bear left to one in a fence. Head away to a stile opposite, and on again to the far end of the field, where a gate reveals Bush Farm. Cross to a stile in a hedge ahead, then bear right to the far corner of the field, left of farm buildings to drop to a corner gate. On a rougher slope, keep right with the fence as far as an old gateway, then drop through a gate into the field below. Descend to the bottom, then go left with the hedge outside the wood to a corner gate near a spring. Just yards further a gate on the right enters the woodland of Mickley Barrass.

A level path heads off to meet a broad one: turn left for a splendid stride through trees. Ignoring a thinner branch rising left, forge on through a bracken clearing above a pool. Dropping down, a stream is crossed into the Woodland Trust's Hackfall Woods. 18th century follies and grottoes by William Aislabie of Studley Royal have recently been restored. A sustained mercurial section closer to the Ure has steep banks above: after a stream crossing, with an island in the river alongside, three ways depart. From the central one stone steps climb to a folly: a lintel carved 'WA 1730' recalls Aislabie.

Take the broad path continuing away along the neck of land, at once joined by the earlier left branch. At a fork a little further, remain on the main right branch to a staggered crossroads, with a branch doubling back left. Instead cross the stream in front, and another fork. The left branch offers a two-minute detour as a super path rises to another folly, this of rougher hewn blocks by a pond. Back at the fork the lower path runs on, dropping to absorb the earlier lower path and around a big river bend. Just beyond, the public path is signed uncertainly left, as a thinner path rising up the bank away from the broad riverside way: they soon re-unite. The upper path does a neat zigzag featuring stone steps onto Limehouse Hill, revealing the river backed by Masham church spire.

A little further the broader path rejoins to run to a corner of the wood. Ignore a kissing-gate ahead and take a path rising left to a gate out of the wood. A fine ascent of a long pasture ultimately reaches a gate from where a track rises to a road. Go briefly left and take a forest track right, rising slightly with a wall to the left. It becomes firmer and bears away from the wall as open pasture is seen over the wall. Turn left here, and within yards a thin path shadows the wall through a trough beneath a newly-planted bank. It remains by the wall until a gate in it just beyond a corner. Leaving the trees a slender trod slants left up a scrubby bank to a stile, through which rise a short way with the hedge then take a stile in it. To the left is an OS column at 705ft/215m on Horsepasture Hill, with the bank of an ancient enclosure visible. A path slants diagonally down to a stile opposite, then down again to another stile. A final field is crossed to the opposite corner, if ploughed possibly keeping left with the wall past a house and around to a stile onto a road. Go left to the village edge, bearing right at a sloping green by the old smithy.

Village pond, Grewelthorpe

*4¼ miles
from West Tanfield*

**Easy rambling by the Ure
from a charming village**

Start **Village centre
(GR: 269788), car park**
Map **OS Explorer 298, Nidderdale**

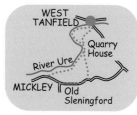

West Tanfield is best viewed from its bridge on the Ure:
dating from around 1734, this fine three-arched structure is an
impressive gateway into the village. St Nicholas' church dates back
to the 14th century, though much restored. Among its tombs are
effigies of Sir John Marmion and his wife from around 1400.
Alongside is the Marmion Tower, 600-year old gatehouse to a long-
disappeared manor house. In the care of English Heritage, spiral
steps lead to the first floor to look over the village. By the bridge
is the Bull Inn, while at the crossroads is the Bruce Arms with old
stables signage. Adjoining the Methodist Church is its predecessor
bearing a lintel of 1798. There is also a Post office/shop.

Leave by crossing Tanfield Bridge, and if the perilous
stepped stile down its right side doesn't appeal, just begin on the
farm drive! This runs along to Quarry House Farm, where a stile on
the left sends an enclosed green track along its near side into a
field at the rear. With the river to the right, advance to a kissing-
gate into the trees ahead. A good path scales the wooded bank
then runs on the steep flank before dropping back down. The path
runs grandly on to join the river for an excellent stride, and along
to a fork on entering trees: to the left is Old Sleningford Farm.
Take the left branch along the wood edge, over a stone slab on the
stream and out into a field. Advance along the wood edge, and at
the end a stile leads through a pronounced break in the wooded
belt to emerge, revealing part of Mickley ahead. Bear left in park-
like surrounds, a line of trees pointing to the nearest cottages
where a stile admits to a short drive onto the road at the eastern

end. Mickley is a tiny but attractive street village, a riot of spring-time colour. St John's little church has a bell-cote.

Your route turns left away from the village, remaining on this back road for rather longer than a mile: initially rising to a junction keep left, on past an interesting lodge then out into open fields. Dropping gently down, leave at a footpath sign on the left at a bend right into a clump of trees. Though the right of way heads directly across the field to join the hedge on the right, common usage follows a headland path further right along the field edge. At the end the field tapers to a corner alongside woods. A short enclosed spell heads through to a stile into a large pasture. With the woods on your left advance almost to the far end, where a stile puts you into the wood. This reveals a great bend of the river just below, and a little path drops down the few yards to rejoin the out-ward route. Turn right to leave the wood by the kissing-gate, and a super riverbank conclusion can normally be enjoyed courtesy of Tanfield Lodge Estate's permissive route: bear left to follow the river to a stile left of the farm. A path runs through undergrowth onto a flood embankment, then simply traces the river downstream round the wide sweep of Greensit Batts, all the way back to the road at Tanfield Bridge.

The River Ure at West Tanfield

4¹⁄4 miles
from Kirkby Malzeard

A gentle amble through rolling country to a lovely village

Start Village centre (GR: 235743), roadside parking
Map OS Explorer 298, Nidderdale

Kirkby Malzeard is an attractive street village granted a market charter in 1307: the replacement buttercross of 1868 occupies the main crossroads. A circular pinfold stands at one end of the village. On a knoll in the wood behind the village stood the castle of Roger de Mowbray: it was destroyed during a rebellion against Henry II. A 500-year old tower and a Norman doorway remain at St Andrew's church, surrounded by some very old grave-stones. A unique pub name celebrates Henry Jenkins, born in 1500 and who supposedly lived for 169 years. There is a second pub, the Queens Head, a shop and even a chip-shop.

Leave the central cross by heading south on the Galphay road, a footway soon forming. Towards the village edge take a stile on the left and slant diagonally down this large pasture, locating a bridle-gate in the fence below. Maintain this course towards Willow House Farm, slanting to a gate in a tree-lined stream then on to a fence-stile left of the farm. Maintain this line beyond the farm environs to a stile in the hedge ahead. Slant up to the brow, and a waymarker keeps you right at an invisible fork, rising to a brow with West Leas Farm over to the left. Looking back, the church tower peeks out. Advance to a kissing-gate ahead onto the farm drive, which is followed right to meet a road.

Go left along the road with good verges, keeping right at a junction at a grassy triangle. Just a little further fork left on the lesser Winksley road, and within a minute take a stile in the hedge on your left. Rise away to the brow of the field, and look back to a long skyline of Kirkby Malzeard Moor. Diverging from the hedge to a gate/stile ahead, continue with a hedge to a gate at the end. With Plover Hill Farm in front, bear right to a corner stile. Now go left with a hedge to enter a newly-planted enclosure, a path running through it to a gate sending you towards a back road in Galphay. Go a few yards right then left along the road to emerge at the green. Galphay is an attractive village with colourful cottages and gardens. Its large, sloping green sports a tall maypole, while a stream tinkles through a smaller, lower green. A circular pinfold was restored in 2002, and its delightful garden makes the perfect spot for a refreshment break. Sadly the Galphay Inn closed its doors in 2009.

Turn left at the green past the old pub to a sharp bend, where pass through impressive gates to follow the lengthy drive to Braithwaite Hall. The inner grounds are entered at a cattle-grid, with farm buildings to the left. Take the main drive ahead, curving left down to the front of the hall. Architecturally very characterful, its great roof appears to entirely overburden the stone walls.

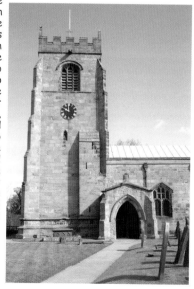

On the right is a large duckpond. In front turn sharp right, as the drive heading away transforms into a green way beneath trees. At the end take the right-hand gate into a large pasture, and keep near the left-hand fence to descend to a gate at the corner. Through it, an access track is joined to lead over Kex Beck to Lawnwith, and its drive followed out to the road at Creets Bridge. Turn left to finish: a snicket immediately after the creamery offers a varied conclusion by way of the churchyard.

Kirkby Malzeard church

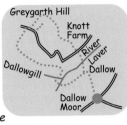

Greygarth Hill
Knott Farm
River Laver
Dallowgill
Dallow
Dallow Moor

4¼ miles from Dallowgill

**Fine walking in a quiet valley
on the fringe of moorland**

*Start Dallow Moor (GR: 199707),
half-mile before Kirkby Malzeard
road crosses cattle-grid to become
confined south of Drovers Inn: parking north of junction
Map OS Explorer 298, Nidderdale*

Just north of the junction a path is signed off left, and
a grassy way slants down the moor. From the outset enjoy a grand
prospect over Dallowgill's diverse pastoral, wooded and moorland
landscapes. At times intermittent the way points down to a stile in a
gate in a corner of the moor. Head down the field, a wall forming to
lead down to a gate onto Dallow's access road. Turn left through the
hamlet to emerge into the open. As the access track swings up to the
left, keep straight on a green way outside the top of a wood. A
colourful mosaic inside it is one of some 22 featuring local scenes
- locations on this walk are indicated thus: (·). The track enters the
trees a little further along to descend steeply to South Gill.

Cross by a footbridge/setted ford, then turn right (·) on
a broader track crossing larger North Gill: their confluence creates
the River Laver. The forest road now climbs steeply right, leaving
the trees but still rising. As it swings sharp right towards a road,
take a stile on the left (·) and cross a field to a gate into woods (·).
A super grassy way runs atop this oakwood, in springtime enjoying
bluebell surrounds to end at a bridle-gate at the far end. Now
below Grey Green Farm, continue on the wallside through the fields
to Bents House (·), and on across two further fields to a derelict
farm ahead. Turn right up its drive onto a moorland road and go
right to a cattle-grid: while the route turns up onto the moor, first
detour over it to a junction with the lane to Dallowgill Methodist
Chapel. A stile on the left sends a thin path up a stony pasture to

Greygarth Monument, erected to commemorate Victoria's Diamond Jubilee. An internal ladder leads to a platform revealing great sweeps of moorland, from those you are fringing to the distant North York Moors. At your feet is the cluster of buildings of Greygarth.

Back at the cattle-grid turn up onto the moor, rising by the wall onto Greygarth Hill. Advance further to descend with the wall, and when it turns off go with it, a vague trod maintaining a course beneath it. Reeds give way to grassier terrain as you advance to the corner. Ignore a grassy way rising towards Greygarth, and take a gate in front. A grass track heads away to the next gate, then down to the far corner of the next field. Through the gate take a wall-stile just past an island barn and follow the wall away to a stile at the end. Now descend a large sloping pasture to a fence-stile on the left just before the bottom. Advance to Knott Farm, dropping to join a track left of the buildings. Pass through the yard and out on the short drive onto a road. A roadside postbox is the only reminder that this was Dallowgill Post office.

With an outdoor centre and a church to the right, cross to a gate into a plantation, and a rough track drops towards the River Laver. At the bottom don't follow the track right, but bear left to a footbridge ahead. Across, a broad path rises right to a bridle-gate out of the trees, then ascend a small enclosure to a gate above. Now rise up the wallside to approach Dallow. A gate to the left admits to a yard: go right, little gates crossing the drive and back up onto the access road. Go briefly left and retrace the opening half-mile up to the start.

Greygarth Monument

41

4¹ 4 miles from Sawley

**Pleasant rural rambling
to lovely wooded lakes**

*Start Village centre (GR:
248677), roadside parking*
Map OS Explorer 298, Nidderdale

Eavestone
Eavestone
Lake

Sawley
Moor
SAWLEY

Sawley is a small village in estate country near Fountains Abbey. St Michael & All Angels' tiny church dates from 1879, on the site of a chapel built by Archbishop Huby of Fountains: across the road is the Sawley Arms. The bell remains on a schoolhouse at the top of the green, now the village hall. From the green follow the access road briefly up its left side, then with the Parish Room of 1900 and a drive on your left, take a wall-stile to rise right up the hedgeside. Up a second field you reach a short-lived hedgerowed path running right to emerge into another field. Resume left up to the top corner, through which is a path crossroads at the end of a rough enclosed lane. Over the stile pass through a gate/stile on your right (you will return to this point) and resume your line, now with a fence on your left. This dead-straight course is maintained through a number of fields, levelling out and on through gates and stiles to the far end where an enclosed path by a shed puts you onto narrow Sawley Moor Lane. Turn right alongside woodland, soon passing through colourful Picking Gill nature reserve. On your right are 19th century quarries, with the natural spring of Wine Wife Well just down to the left. Emerging onto the dead-straight B6265 Pateley Bridge-Ripon road, turn left on some useful verges as far as an escape point down the Eavestone cul-de-sac.

Down past the farm, as the road swings sharp left, drop a little then take a path doubling back into the wood. Here begins a glorious spell on a good path in magnificent surroundings. First feature is the upper reservoir of Eavestone Lake, with a dark crag jutting into the water. The gritstone surrounding these two lakes yields rock climbs of every standard on at least sixteen separate buttresses: some literally overhang the path by the main lake! Across its outflow the path winds round to the head of Eavestone Lake, then runs its full length. Of immediate interest are the forbidding outcrops of Ravens Crag towering above the opposite bank. Waterfowl, springtime bluebells and wild garlic amid the luxuriant foliage of this mixed woodland combine to provide a half-hour of sheer delight.

At the end fork right to cross a small dam and a little arched bridge. Penance for such delights is a sustained pull through Fishpond Wood. A gate at the top consigns the Eavestone scene to memory as you pass round the left side of a field to join the drive to Hollin Hill Farm. Take its drive round to the back, and straight on through a gate into a scrubby corner. Advance into the field corner, and keep to the right to find a ladder-stile into a slim enclosure. As it opens out keep with its right side to run along to West Gowbusk. Go straight through the farmyard and out on the drive, but quickly leave by a private-looking gate on the left. This accesses the front of a cottage at Gowbusk, to follow its drive back out onto the B6265. Go briefly left and take a stile on the right: the houses of Sawley appear ahead.

Cross over the field to a stile in the far corner, then rise gently along the fieldsides. Broad views look across to the distant North York Moors; note also the prominent spire of Studley Royal church and perhaps a glimpse of the tower of Fountains Abbey in the intervening rolling country. Reaching the rough enclosed lane again, take the stile on your left to retrace the opening steps back down into the village.

Eavestone Lake

*4¹2 miles
from Fountains Abbey*

**Elegant walking through a
celebrated deer park and
a delightful little valley**

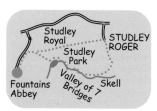

Start **Visitor Centre (GR: 272686), National Trust car park**
Map **OS Explorer 298, Nidderdale (or Explorer 299)**
Access **Open access in deer park**

The National Trust property of Fountains Abbey and Studley Royal is designated a World Heritage Site, its combination of staggeringly beautiful ruins and exquisite water gardens making this a major visitor attraction. Founded in 1132, the abbey forms the most extensive Cistercian remains in England, and its setting in the wooded valley of the River Skell is unsurpassed. The adjacent water gardens with various follies were laid out by the Aislabie family in the 18th century, while 17th century Fountains Hall offers further interest. While this walk visits the 'free' Studley Royal deer park, it is worth making a day of it to savour the 'paying' attractions too.

By the roundabout at the visitor centre entrance, a bridle-way runs through trees parallel with the access road. This emerges by the road at a pedestrian entrance to Studley Park, with a tall obelisk of 1815 dwarfed by St Mary's church. Through the gate pass the obelisk and advance to the church, built in 1871-78 and boasting an impressive great spire prominent in many views around the neighbourhood. It is open on afternoons from Easter to October. From opposite the door a grassy path descends to the abbey's east entrance by the lake. Here is a shop, tearoom, WCs and a ticket office for entry to the abbey and water gardens.

Follow the drive left alongside the lake, and at the end remain on a track to the outflow. Here begins the walk through the Valley of Seven Bridges, the first being a wooden one over the out-flowing River Skell. This is accompanied downstream through the encroaching walls of this steep-sided valley, a delightful amble that re-crosses the river on five further occasions, each by means of identical stone-arched bridges. The river disappears underground part way along. After the last one the estate is vacated at a tall gate, and a woodland path runs down to pass the seventh bridge (a plain structure not crossed) before the track climbs the wooded bank to leave the river. Out of the trees it runs a pleasant fieldside course with open views featuring Ripon Cathedral little more than a stone's throw away, with a long line of the Hambleton Hills beyond.

Passing mellow-walled Plumpton Hall and attendant farm buildings, the track becomes surfaced to reach the edge of Studley Roger at a lodge and small green. This unassuming village features attractive cottages with red pantile roofs. Look right along the carriageway which forms a perfect alignment with cathedral and church. Go left on the estate drive, through the East Entrance arch to re-enter the park. Strolling along the broad driveway, St Mary's church is framed beyond a long avenue of limes. In the heart of the centuries-old deer park many of these creatures can be discerned, the three breeds present being Red deer, Fallow deer and Sika deer, introduced from Manchuria in the 1600s. When cars are sent left to the car park above the lake, remain on the drive to the church and retrace steps to the visitor centre.

The Lake, Studley Park

3¹2 miles from Ripon

Uncomplicated riverbank walking on the edge of an absorbing tiny city

Start North Bridge (GR: 317720), roadside parking

Map OS Explorer 299, Ripon & Boroughbridge

Yorkshire's smallest city is dominated by a beautiful cathedral on the site of Wilfrid's 7th century monastery: a Saxon crypt survives. The present Cathedral dates from the late 12th century, with later additions. The West front presents a stunning high wall filling the end of Kirkgate, internal delights include the East window and a medieval screen. The market square present a lively scene on Thursdays: centrepiece is a tall obelisk of 1702. For many centuries a 'Wakeman' was responsible for the townsfolk's safety during darkness hours, and this setting of the watch was heralded by the sounding of a horn, a millennium-old tradition maintained at 9pm. Overlooking the square is the Town Hall of 1801, while the Wakeman's House with its Tudor facade is just doors away. Many central street names are still 'gates' and the layout has changed little since medieval times. Other buildings of interest are Cathedral Hall on the site of a medieval school, with the red-brick Old Hall of 1738 in Minster Close. The Law & Order Museums occupy gaunt Victorian surroundings, while the Ripon Canal links to the River Ure.

Where Magdalen's Road meets the main road turn right over the elegant arches of North Bridge, then bear right to shadow the Ure under the modern by-pass. On the other side a path clings to the river alongside Sharow Lane: as the road quickly turns off join it, following its footway past an old milestone and rising gently to a fork at Sharow Cross. This 13th century sanctuary cross is the last survivor of eight that gave privilege to fugitives within a mile of the city centre: it also boasts a view of the cathedral. Bear right here on the narrower Sharow Lane, pleasantly along the edge of the village to drop down to a grassy triangle. Just a little further along is the Half Moon Inn, with St John's church further back.

Turn right on a track which runs a delightful hedgerowed course: an early glance back reveals the church overtopping a neat village scene. Towards the end it becomes grassier to emerge into a field alongside a wood. A path continues, and beyond the wood end runs to a bridle-gate in the hedge. Strike across the field centre to join an embanked riverbank path. While your onward route is right, a brief diversion left to Hewick Bridge reveals the concrete remains of a ford used by tanks during Second World War training. Turning upstream, the path runs an uncomplicated course by the Ure, sometimes through scrub, often on the true wooded bank, all the way to emerge back alongside Sharow Lane where you left it near the start. Conclude by retracing steps back under the by-pass.

Left: Sharow church   *The Ure at Ripon*

HILLSIDE GUIDES... cover much of Northern England

Other colour *Pocket Walks* guides (more in preparation)
·UPPER WHARFEDALE ·LOWER WHARFEDALE
·UPPER WENSLEYDALE ·LOWER WENSLEYDALE
·MALHAMDALE ·SWALEDALE ·RIBBLESDALE
·INGLETON/WESTERN DALES ·SEDBERGH/DENTDALE
·NIDDERDALE ·HARROGATE/KNARESBOROUGH
·BOWLAND ·AROUND PENDLE ·RIBBLE VALLEY
·AMBLESIDE/LANGDALE ·BORROWDALE
·AIRE VALLEY ·ILKLEY/WASHBURN VALLEY

Our *Walking Country* range features more great walks...

·WHARFEDALE ·MALHAMDALE ·WENSLEYDALE
·HARROGATE & the WHARFE VALLEY ·SWALEDALE
·RIPON & LOWER WENSLEYDALE ·NIDDERDALE
·THREE PEAKS ·HOWGILL FELLS ·HOWARDIAN HILLS
·TEESDALE ·EDEN VALLEY ·ALSTON & ALLENDALE

·ILKLEY MOOR ·BRONTE COUNTRY ·CALDERDALE
·PENDLE & the RIBBLE ·WEST PENNINE MOORS
·ARNSIDE & SILVERDALE ·LUNESDALE ·BOWLAND

·LAKELAND FELLS, SOUTH ·LAKELAND FELLS, EAST
·LAKELAND FELLS, NORTH ·LAKELAND FELLS, WEST

Long Distance Walks
·COAST TO COAST WALK ·CUMBRIA WAY ·DALES WAY
·LADY ANNE'S WAY ·NIDDERDALE WAY
·WESTMORLAND WAY ·FURNESS WAY
·PENDLE WAY ·BRONTE WAY ·CALDERDALE WAY

Visit www.hillsidepublications.co.uk
or write for a catalogue